D1738131

Donald Trump's Book of Lies

By

Samuel G. Allen

Most of us know the story of George Washington and his hatchet, first told by biographer Mason Locke Weems, sometimes doubted but never disproven, in which the young Washington claims "I cannot tell a lie," and is richly rewarded for it. Since that time truthfulness has been touted to young children as a trait of character needed to rise to a station of high esteem. How things have changed! Today we have a president who has risen to that office largely on a bed of lies. Exposing these lies is so widely done that today's children cannot be unaware of them. How can we expect them to tell the truth with an example such as this? Rather than tell the truth, say whatever puts you in the best light! Such an example cannot but create problems for both parents and teachers and could shake the foundation of our society.

Very few of Donald Trump's misstatements are controversial. The great majority is easily disproven and fall into one of four categories:

A. Self-aggrandizing statements, such as overstating his Electoral College win and the size of the crowds at his inauguration and at his rallies.

B. Claiming credit for things he had nothing or very little to do with.

C. Denying that he said or did things that are on the record or which he previously had admitted to.

D. Misstatements made to push an agenda, such as saying that U. S. unemployment is at a historic high when in fact there is a labor shortage; or implying that there is no wall along the U. S. – Mexico border and illegal immigrants are pouring in. During the campaign the Republican Party even screened a video of such an occurrence, made in Morocco.

Here is a selective collection of Donald Trump's misstatements from the time of his election in November of 2016 to the time of publication. The first of these are from Politico Magazine and the later ones are from such sources as The New York Times, The Washington Post, and Politifact, whom Donald Trump characterizes as purveyors of "fake news" because they print the truth about him.

Nov 13, 2016 (Twitter): "Wow, the @nytimes is losing thousands of subscribers because of their very poor and highly inaccurate coverage of the 'Trump phenomena'"

The Times reports that between Election Day and Trump's tweet, the paper added four times the average number of net new digital and print subscriptions.

Nov 13, 2016 (Twitter) "The @nytimes states today that DJT believes 'more countries should acquire nuclear weapons.' How dishonest are they. I never said this!"

In a May 4, 2016 interview with Wolf Blitzer, Donald Trump was asked if he is ready to let Japan and South Korea become nuclear powers. Trump responded, "I am prepared to, if they're not going to take care of us properly, we cannot afford to be the military and police for the world." On March 29, 2016, Anderson Cooper asked Trump, "Saudi Arabia, nuclear weapons?" Trump replied, "Saudi Arabia, absolutely."

Nov 17, 2016 (Twitter) "Just got a call from my friend Bill Ford, Chairman of Ford, who advised me that he will be keeping the Lincoln plant in Kentucky - no Mexico [...] I worked hard with Bill Ford to keep the Lincoln plant in Kentucky. I owed it to the great State of Kentucky for their confidence in me!"

Ford never had any plans to move its Kentucky plant or fire any of its employees there. According to a Reuters report, the plan was to move its production line of Lincoln SUVs from a Kentucky facility to Mexico, and then to direct the workers at that Kentucky plant to begin building Ford Escapes. At no point were American jobs at risk.

Nov 20, 2016 (The New York Times) "The last [campaign rally] ended at 1 o'clock in the morning in Michigan. And we had 31,000 people, 17,000 or 18,000 inside and the rest outside."

Police told Breitbart News that they estimated 6,000 people attended Trump's final campaign rally at the DeVos center in Grand Rapids, Michigan.

Nov 20, 2016 (The New York Times) "We ended up close to 15 points of the African American vote, as you know."

Donald Trump received approximately 8 percent of the black vote, according to polling data. Obama won 96% of the black vote in 2008.

Nov 20, 2016 (The New York Times) "First of all, we don't make the windmills in the United States. They're made in Germany and Japan."

A report from the Energy Department said 72 percent of wind turbine equipment installed in the United States in 2012 was made by domestic manufacturers.

Nov 27, 2016 (Twitter) "In addition to winning the Electoral College in a landslide, I won the popular vote if you deduct the millions of people who voted illegally"

This may refer to a Washington Post article from 2014 that used data from the Cooperative Congressional Election Study to assert large numbers of non-citizens voted in the 2008 and 2010 elections. The article was highly contested, including through three rebuttals and a peer-reviewed article arguing that the methodology of the original article was flawed.

Nov 27, 2016 (Twitter) "Serious voter fraud in Virginia, New Hampshire and California - so why isn't the media reporting on this? Serious bias - big problem!"

Politifact investigated this claim in all three states mentioned, and rated Trump's claim "Pants on Fire" in each case. Secretaries of state in California and New Hampshire told Politifact that Trump's allegation is unfounded and baseless, and Virginia's top election official said the same.

Dec 1, 2016 (Cincinnati, Ohio) "We have no idea who [Middle East refugees accepted in the United States] are, where they come from."

According to the State Department, the review process for refugees takes an average of 18-24 months to complete. That process includes two in-depth interviews, security screenings by at least five national security agencies and biometric security checks. The government has a very good idea of who refugees are and where they come from by the time they reach U.S. soil.

Dec 1, 2016 (Cincinnati, Ohio) "And today, you're older and you're working harder. And in many cases, you have two jobs. Some of that is because of Obamacare."

According to the Bureau of Labor Statistics, when Obama took office in 2009, 5.2 percent of the workforce held multiple jobs. That number dropped down to 5.0 in 2010, when Obamacare was passed, and then dropped to 4.9 percent between 2011 and 2015. In the first 11 months of 2016, that number rose back to 5.0 percent, the same as it was in 2010.

Dec 8, 2016 (Des Moines, Iowa) "We got to get the jobs. We got 96 million people out there."

Trump likely meant 94 million people, the total number of Americans age 16 and over who aren't in the labor force. That number, however, includes all retirees, stay-at-home parents, people with disabilities who aren't working, people who can afford to work and choose not to and high school and college students. The most common unemployment number used by the Bureau of Labor Statistics (U-3), counted approximately 7.4 million Americans in November. An alternative BLS measure (U-6), which includes people who looked for a job for an entire year but gave up and part-time employees who would prefer full-time work, counts nearly 15 million Americans. That's a fraction of the 96 million that Trump suggests are seeking jobs.

Dec 9, 2016 (Baton Rouge, Louisiana) "We haven't had refineries built in decades, right? We're going to have refineries built again."

According to the U.S. Energy Information Administration, two petroleum refineries were built in Texas in 2015, and in 2014, one was built in Texas and one in North Dakota.

Dec 9, 2016 (Grand Rapids, Michigan) "Now, I get no credit for this. [The Clinton campaign] spent $2.2 billion [in Michigan]. What did we spend? Like, a little more than $300 million."

In any consistent accounting method, Trump is overestimating Hillary Clinton's spending. According to the final numbers from the Federal Election Commission, if one includes groups allied with the campaigns, Clinton spent about $1.2 billion in Michigan, while Trump and his allies spent about $600 million. If you limit the accounting to funds spent by the campaign, the totals drop to around $562 million spent by the Clinton campaign and $313 million by the Trump campaign.

Dec 11, 2016 "We had a massive landslide victory, as you know, in the Electoral College."

The percentage of Electoral College votes Trump won—56.88 percent—ranks in the bottom quartile of the nation's 54 presidential elections. In the 18 elections since the end of World War II, Trump's percentage ranks in the bottom third.

Dec 11, 2016 "You look at what's happening in Mexico, where are people just, our plants are being built, and they don't wait 10 years to get an approval to build a plant, they build it, like, the following day or the following week."

According to Alejandro Orozco, a consultant in Mexico City with FTI Consulting, it can be quite difficult for major companies to get the environmental permits to begin construction in Mexico. "You are required to prove the environmental impact of your project," The process to get the federal permit usually takes a year, he said, and can be longer than that for big projects. "I doubt that you can get the proper permits in less than six months."

Dec 12, 2016 (Twitter) "Unless you catch 'hackers' in the act, it is very hard to determine who was doing the hacking." Trump's tweet is part of his argument that Russia's role in election hacking remains unknown.

First, CrowdStrike, the cybersecurity firm that initially connected the Democratic National Committee hack to the Russian government, did catch the hackers in the act. "When the DNC hired us back in May, we actually came in and deployed our technology, called Falcon, on all of the systems inside their corporate network," Dmitri Alperovitch, a co-founder of CrowdStrike, told CNN's Wolf Blitzer in December. "We actually watched these adversaries for a number of days and weeks as we were preparing to kick them out."

Even if the DNC hackers had not been caught in the act, Trump is wrong to assert that investigators could no longer determine their identities. In the DNC's case, Alperovitch wrote on the company's blog that they recognized malicious codes and hacking techniques unique to two Russian-connected actors: "Cozy Bear" and "Fancy Bear."

Cybersecurity experts connected both of these actors to the Russian government years ago. Not only do their hacking operations—whose targets have included the White House, NATO and the World Anti-Doping Agency—dovetail with Russian state interests, but investigators have found the malware used by these actors was built with Russian language settings, was largely compiled during Moscow's and St. Petersburg's working hours, can be traced back to Russian IP addresses and required an amount of dedicated resources usually associated with nation-states.

Both the private experts and public intelligence officials agree: Cozy Bear and Fancy Bear hacked the DNC, and the operation was almost certainly directed by the Russian government.

Dec 15, 2016 (Twitter) "If Russia, or some other entity, was hacking, why did the White House wait so long to act? Why did they only complain after Hillary lost?"

On October 7, a month before Election Day, the Obama administration officially accused the Russian government of deploying hackers to meddle with the U.S. election. "The U.S. Intelligence Community (USIC) is confident that the Russian Government directed the recent compromises of e-mails from US persons and institutions, including from US Political organizations," the Department of Homeland Security and Office of the Director of National Intelligence on Election Security announced in a joint statement. "These thefts and disclosures are intended to interfere with the US election process." Four days later, White House Press Secretary Josh Earnest promised that the United States would deliver a "proportional" response.

Dec 15, 2016 (Hershey, Pa.) "The murder rate in the United States is the largest that it's been in 45 years."

The murder rate in 2015 was 4.9 murders per 100,000 people. The murder rate over the past 45-year period peaked in 1980, when it hit 10.2 murders per 100,000 people—more than double the current rate. The lowest murder rate over the past 51 years was reached in 2014: 4.5 murders per 100,000 people.

Dec 17, 2016 (Mobile, Ala.) "People that come into the country illegally, people that come into the country and cause problems, they're taken care of better than our vets in many cases."

This is a statement Trump repeatedly made during the campaign and that was repeatedly refuted by the fact-checkers at Politifact, Factcheck.org and the Washington Post. They concluded that by virtually no standard are veterans treated worse than undocumented immigrants. This is true for medical care, public benefits eligibility, legal treatment by the government and more.

Dec 26, 2016 (Twitter) "The DJT Foundation, unlike most foundations, never paid fees, rent, salaries or any expenses. 100% of money goes to wonderful charities!"

The Trump Foundation's latest report to the IRS admitted to "self-dealing," which means the charity transferred income or assets to someone it wasn't allowed to, per IRS rules. This followed reporting by David A. Fahrenthold of the Washington Post, who revealed that Trump used $258,000 from the foundation to settle legal problems afflicting his for-profit businesses. Fahrenthold also reported that in 2007, Trump used $20,000 from his charity to purchase a six-foot-tall portrait of himself. Half the money went to charity, and the other half went to the painter.

Jan 7, 2017 (Twitter) "Intelligence stated very strongly there was absolutely no evidence that hacking affected the election results. Voting machines not touched!"

The intelligence report Trump is referring to stated that Russia did target voting machines but did not compromise the final tally. The report did not say, however, that Russia didn't affect the election's outcome. The report said explicitly, "We did not make an assessment of the impact that Russian activities had on the outcome of the 2016 election."

Jan 9, 2017 (The New York Times) "All the dress shops are sold out in Washington. It's hard to find a great dress for this inauguration."

After this comments, Washingtonian magazine canvassed D.C.'s local dress shops. None reported a shortage in dresses or expected there would be any time soon.

Jan 11, 2017 "I'm not releasing the tax returns because, as you know, they're under audit."

For 12 months, Trump has made claims about why he won't release his returns, sometimes citing his audit, and sometimes citing the advice of his lawyer. But there is no law that prevents the release of tax returns under audit. In fact, in 1973, Richard Nixon released his tax returns despite being under an IRS audit at the time.

Jan 11, 2017 "Nobody has ever had crowds like Trump has had."

Although Trump did draw very large crowds during the campaign, he often exaggerated their size, and his rallies rarely exceeded 15,000 attendees. His largest rally was likely in August 2015, when Trump attracted 30,000 people in Mobile, Alabama. For comparison, 100,000 people attended an Obama rally in October 2008, when he visited St. Louis. Obama drew approximately 72,000 people for a rally in Portland, Oregon, in 2007, and 35,000 turned out for one of his rallies in Philadelphia.

Jan 11, 2017 "Russia has never tried to use leverage over me. I HAVE NOTHING TO DO WITH RUSSIA - NO DEALS, NO LOANS, NO NOTHING!"

Because Trump has not released his tax returns, there is a lot we don't know about Trump's business abroad. However, there is evidence to suggest that Trump has done business with Russian investors, at least in the past. The Washington Post reported that at a real estate conference in 2008, Donald Trump Jr. said that "Russians make up a pretty disproportionate cross-section of a lot of our assets." He then added, "We see a lot of money pouring in from Russia." Additionally, POLITICO's Michael Crowley has reported on Trump's business connections to several wealthy Russians. In 2013, when Trump brought the Miss Universe pageant to Moscow in 2013, he developed a friendly relationship with the Russian billionaire and real estate mogul Aras Agalarov. And back in 2004, Trump sold a $100 million home to Russian oligarch Dmitry Rybolovlev.

Jan 19, 2017 "It's called we want our children educated. That's our take. So we're number one in the world in cost per pupil. Number one in the world."

According to statistics from the OECD, the United States ranks sixth in the world for spending per pupil in secondary education and fifth in the world for spending per pupil in primary education.

Jan 21, 2017 "I have been on the cover of Time Magazine 14 or 15 times. I think we have the all-time record in the history of Time magazine."

Trump was on the cover 11 times and Nixon appeared 55 times.

Jan 25, 2017 "Now, the audience [at his inauguration] was the biggest ever. But this crowd was massive. Look how far back it goes. This crowd was massive."

Official photos show Obama's 2009 inauguration was much more heavily attended.

Above: Barack Obama' inauguration in 2009

Below: Donald Trump's Inauguration in 2017

Jan. 26, 2017 "I cut off hundreds of millions of dollars off one particular plane, hundreds of millions of dollars in a short period of time. It wasn't like I spent, like, weeks, hours, less than hours, and many, many hundreds of millions of dollars.

Trump, yet again, claims credit for decisions that were already made before he became president. Trump stated he "was able to get $600 million approximately off those planes," thereby ending the "difficulty" and "no movement" in the program. Yet the Pentagon had already announced cost reductions of roughly $600 million before Trump began meeting with Lockheed Martin's chief executive.

Jan 29, 2017 "The Cuban-Americans, I got 84 percent of that vote."

According to the Pew Research Center, Trump got 54% of the Cubano vote.

Feb 24, 2017 "By the way, you folks are in here — this place is packed, there are lines that go back six blocks." President Trump falsely claimed during his speech at the Conservative Political Action Conference.

It was a statement at odds with the quiet scene outside the Gaylord National Resort and Convention Center, where CPAC was taking place. There were no lines getting into the Gaylord within the hour before Trump began speaking Friday morning.

The entire National Harbor development along the Potomac River stretches about six blocks. Streets surrounding the area were quiet save for a few people, mostly CPAC volunteers, stopping at a nearby Starbucks and security officers patrolling the front of the Gaylord. Trump spent a significant part of his speech bashing a news media that he thinks isn't giving him enough positive coverage.

Feb 24, 2017 "We've defended other nations' borders while leaving ours wide open, anybody can come in."

The United States apprehended 415,816 people in the 2016 fiscal year, so hundreds of thousands of people did not just "come in."

Under the country's visa waiver program, citizens from some 30 countries are allowed to enter the United States without a visa for up to 90 days. Citizens from other countries must apply for a visa and could be rejected; waiting times vary. Refugees who are referred to resettlement in the United States typically wait up to two years.

Feb 24, 2017 "Obamacare covers very few people. And remember, deduct from the number all of those people who had great health care that they loved that was taken away from them."

About 20 million people have gained coverage under the Affordable Care Act, and the uninsured rate has dropped to a record low of 10.9 percent.

The left-leaning Urban Institute estimated that 2.6 million plans were canceled because they did not meet minimum requirements set by the act. But fewer than one million people ended up with no insurance at all, and it is not clear that this was entirely attributable to health care law.

Feb 27, 2017 "Since Obamacare went into effect, nearly half of the insurers are stopped and have stopped from participating in the Obamacare exchanges."

Contradicting the New York Times, our calculations support Trump's estimate.

Mar 4, 2017 (Twitter) "Terrible! Just found out that Obama had my 'wires tapped' in Trump Tower just before the victory. Nothing found. This is McCarthyism!"

A bizarre accusation not supported by any evidence.

Mar 7, 2017 (Twitter) "122 vicious prisoners, released by the Obama Administration from Gitmo, have returned to the battlefield. Just another terrible decision!"

According to the Office of the Director of National Intelligence, of the 714 former Guantánamo Bay detainees who were transferred to other countries by Jan. 15, 2017 — dating back to when the Bush administration opened the prison in Cuba in January 2002 — 121 are "confirmed" to have engaged in militant activity after their release, however, the overwhelming majority of those 121 men, 113 of them, were transferred under President George W. Bush, not President Barack Obama.

Mar 22, 2017 "NATO, obsolete, because it doesn't cover terrorism.

At its peak, NATO and its partners sent about 40,000 troops to Afghanistan, and this year, there are still about 4,000 troops from NATO allies in Afghanistan.

Apr 12, 2017 (Fox News) "What I did [in Syria] should have been done by the Obama administration a long time before I did it and you would have had a much better — I think Syria would be a lot better off right now than it has been."

In 2013 and 2014, Trump repeatedly tweeted against Obama launching air attacks against Syria for allegedly deploying chemical weapons. Trump repeated this in more than a dozen tweets, saying Obama should "stay the hell out of Syria," and that it would be "stupid" and that "very bad things will happen." He urged Obama to instead "fix U.S.A." and "focus on making our country strong and great again."

Apr 13, 2017 "If you look at what's happened over the last eight weeks and compare that really to what's happened over the last eight years, you'll see there's a tremendous difference — tremendous difference."

During a meeting with emergency medical workers, Mr. Trump boasted that he had done more against the Islamic State than Mr. Obama had in a fraction of the time. Under the Obama administration, a military coalition recaptured several major cities from the Islamic State and launched more than 17,000 airstrikes in Iraq and Syria. Since Mr. Trump's inauguration, the Islamic State had lost no major cities, and the coalition had conducted about 2,000 airstrikes.

Apr 16, 2017 "Someone should look into who paid for the small organized rallies yesterday. The election is over!"

Tens of thousands across the country took to the streets as part of Tax March to demand Mr. Trump's tax returns, which he has not released. Ezra Levin, a member of Tax March's executive committee, called Mr. Trump's tweet "bogus and flat-out false."

Apr 17, 2017 "The fake media goes, 'Donald Trump changed his stance on China.' I haven't changed my stance."

During the 2016 campaign, Mr. Trump repeatedly promised to declare China a currency manipulator, and he labeled China that in an interview with The Financial Times in early April. But he told The Wall Street Journal later that month that he would no longer do so.

Apr 18, 2017 "The weak illegal immigration policies of the Obama Admin. allowed bad MS-13 gangs to form in cities across U.S. We are removing them fast!"

MS-13, precedes Mr. Obama's presidency by decades. By 2005, four years before Mr. Obama took office, the F.B.I. reported that MS-13 had 10,000 "hardcore members" active, the same number cited by Attorney General Jeff Sessions on the day of Mr. Trump's claim.

MS-13 is an international criminal gang that originated in Los Angeles, California, US in the 1980s. The gang later spread to many parts of the continental United States, Canada, Mexico, and Central America, and is active in urban and suburban areas. Most members are of Central American origin, principally El Salvador.

Originally the gang's main purpose was to protect Salvadoran immigrants from other, more established gangs of Los Angeles, who were predominantly composed of Mexicans and African-Americans.

Apr 21, 2017 "I saved $725 million on the 90 planes. Just 90. Now there are 3,000 planes that are going to be ordered. On 90 planes I saved $725 million. It's actually a little bit more than that, but it's $725 million."

Trump keeps claiming he saved hundreds of millions of dollars on the cost of the F-35 Joint Strike Fighter planes by intervening in negotiations with Lockheed Martin. But Lockheed already had planned cost reductions, and Trump overstates his role. In a Dec. 19 briefing — before Trump began meeting with Lockheed's chief executive Marillyn Hewson — the head of the Defense Department's F-35 Joint Program Office announced costs would come down "significantly." The average unit price for the planes has been declining for years, and the Pentagon had wanted to reduce costs further. The cost savings for the latest batch of planes was projected to be between $549 million and $630 million for a full lot of 90 planes. The Pentagon announced that the total savings from the program will be $728 million.

Apr 24, 2017 "The Wall is a very important tool in stopping drugs from pouring into our country and poisoning our youth (and many others)! If ... the wall is not built, which it will be, the drug situation will NEVER be fixed the way it should be!"

Mr. Trump's border wall would not address several modes of drug trafficking from Mexican criminal networks. According to the Drug Enforcement Administration's 2016 report, the most common method of transporting drugs is in concealed compartments in vehicles crossing ports of entry. Other methods rely on tunnels, drones and commercial cargo trains and buses.

None of these methods would be prevented by a wall.

Apr 25, 2017 "Virtually every country has a surplus with the United States."

There are at least a dozen countries that have trade deficits with the United States, including Australia, Netherlands, Belgium, Brazil and Egypt.

Apr 25, 2017 "You live by the sword; you die by the sword, to a certain extent. But we create a lot of jobs, 500,000 jobs as of two months ago, and plenty created since. Five hundred thousand. ... As an example, Ford, General Motors. I've had cases where the gentleman from China, Ma, Jack Ma (chairman of Alibaba Group), he comes up, he says, 'Only because of you am I making this massive investment.' Intel, only because of you. ... The press never writes that."

Trump likes to claim undue credit for corporate decisions that were made before he was elected president. And Trump exaggerates the number of jobs created since he became president; the number of net new jobs since January 2017 is 317,000. Ford's decision to expand in Michigan rather than in Mexico had more to do with the company's long-term goals than with the administration. Ford outlined these goals in a contract it negotiated with the United Auto Workers in 2015.

General Motors announced job plans in January and March 2017, but the company did not credit Trump or his election. Intel announced it would create at least 10,000 jobs at a "new" plant in Arizona. The company announced its investment in this factory in 2011 with President Barack Obama, but it never opened. Intel is resuming its factory project because it anticipates a demand in computer chips that will be created there. As for the Chinese e-company Alibaba, its founder Jack Ma has been pitching his company as a U.S. job creator since as early as 2015.

April 25, 2017 "I am very upset with NAFTA. I think NAFTA has been a catastrophic trade deal for the United States, trading agreement for the United States. It hurts us with Canada, and it hurts us with Mexico. Most people don't even think of NAFTA in terms of Canada. You saw what happened yesterday in my statements, because if you look at the dairy farmers in Wisconsin and upstate New York, they are getting killed by NAFTA."

It is often difficult to separate out the impact of trade agreements on jobs, compared to other, broader economic trends. But the nonpartisan Congressional Research Service in 2015 concluded that the "net overall effect of NAFTA on the U.S. economy appears to have been relatively modest, primarily because trade with Canada and Mexico accounts for a small percentage of U.S. GDP," though it noted "there were worker and firm adjustment costs as the three countries adjusted to more open trade and investment among their economies."

As for farmers in Wisconsin being "killed" by NAFTA, Canadian dairy products are actually not covered by NAFTA, as that industry is protected from U.S. exports and remains under "supply management" (price controls) which results in high retail prices in Canada. Canadian consumers basically subsidize farmers; by contrast, American dairy producers receive subsidies from the U.S. government.

Apr 28, 2017 "The trade deficit with Mexico is close to $70 billion, even with Canada it's $17 billion trade deficit with Canada."

The U.S. had an $8.1 billion trade surplus, not deficit, with Canada in 2016.

May 5, 2017 "We pay the highest taxes anywhere in the world."

Data from 2014, the most recent year available, shows that the United States wasn't the most highly taxed by the typical metrics and actually places near the bottom or around the middle of the pack. Trump specified this time that he was talking about business taxes, but the essential data doesn't back him there, either. The United States does have one of the highest top marginal corporate tax rates in the world. However, companies pay less in practice because they can take deductions and exclusions. When we look at the actual tax burden on U.S. companies, it's far from highest in the world.

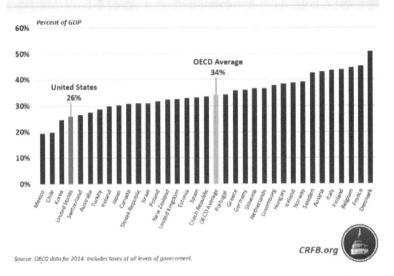

U.S. Among Lowest-Taxed Countries in the OECD

Source: OECD data for 2014. Includes taxes at all levels of government.

CRFB.org

May 12, 2017 "Again, the story that there was collusion between the Russians & Trump campaign was fabricated by Dems as an excuse for losing the election."

The F.B.I. was investigating before the election.

Jun 1, 2017 "China will be allowed to build hundreds of additional coal plants. So, we can't build the plants, but they can, according to this agreement. India will be allowed to double its coal production by 2020."

The agreement is nonbinding and each nation sets its own targets. There is nothing in the agreement that stops the United States from building coal plants or gives the permission to China or India to build coal plants. In fact, market forces, primarily reduced costs for natural gas, have forced the closure of coal plants. China announced this year that it would cancel plans to build more than 100 coal-fired plants.

"China will be able to increase these emissions by a staggering number of years, 13. They can do whatever they want for 13 years. India makes its participation contingent on receiving billions and billions and billions of dollars in foreign aid from developed countries."

China, in its Paris Accord commitment, said that, compared to 2005 levels, it would seek to cut its carbon emissions by 60 to 65 percent per unit of GDP by 2030. India said it would reduce its emissions per unit of economic output by 33 to 35 percent below 2005 by 2030; the submission does seek foreign aid to meet its goals and mitigate the costs.

June 21, 2017 "And we've ended the war on clean, beautiful coal. And we're putting our miners back to work. In fact, you read about it, last week a brand new coal mine just opened in the state of Pennsylvania, first time in decades, decades. We've reversed – and 33,000 mining jobs have been added since my inauguration."

In fact, there has been an increase of about 1,000 coal mining jobs since January, according to the Bureau of Labor Statistics. For some perspective, there has been a total loss of nearly 40,000 coal mining jobs over the last five years. How does Trump get to 33,000? After talking specifically about coal mining, Trump cites a figure for all mining jobs – including gas, oil, metal ores, coal and nonmetallic mineral mining and quarrying. There have been 32,600 total mining jobs added since January.

As for the grand opening of the Corsa Coal Company's Acosta Deep Mine near Pittsburgh on June 8, that had nothing to do with Trump's efforts to roll back coal regulations. As we wrote when Trump made similar boasts earlier this month, development of the Acosta mine began in September, two months before Trump's election victory. Industry experts also tell us it is not emblematic of a resurgence of coal mining.

The Acosta mine produces a particular type of coal that is used to make steel. That's a bit of a niche market in the coal industry, accounting for just 10 percent of coal production in the U.S.

There has been a surge in demand for this kind of coal because of production problems overseas. However, the vast majority of coal produced in the U.S. is thermal coal, the kind used to generate electricity. Consumption of that kind of coal has declined by nearly 18 percent between 2012 and 2016, mostly due to the surge in cheaper natural gas production driven by the shale revolution and to competition from renewable energy.

July 17, 2017 "We've signed more bills — and I'm talking about through the legislature — than any president, ever."

At the time he said it, Mr. Trump had signed 42 bills, and it was not a record. President Jimmy Carter signed 70 bills in the first six months, according to an analysis of bills signed by previous White House occupants. Bill Clinton signed 50. George W. Bush signed 20 bills into law. Barack Obama signed 39 bills during that period. Harry Truman and Franklin Delano Roosevelt both had signed more bills into law by their 100-day mark than Mr. Trump did in almost twice that time. Harry Truman had signed 55 bills and Roosevelt had signed 76 during their first 100 days.

Jul 19, 2017 "[Hillary Clinton] did the uranium deal, which is a horrible thing, while she was secretary of state, and got a lot of money."

On June 8, 2010, Uranium One announced it had signed an agreement that would give "not less than 51%" of the company to JSC Atomredmetzoloto, or ARMZ, the mining arm of Rosatom, the Russian nuclear energy agency.

At the time, Uranium One's two licensed mining operations in Wyoming amounted to about "20 percent of the currently licensed uranium in-situ recovery production capacity in the U.S.," according to the Nuclear Regulatory Commission. In-situ recovery is the extraction method currently used by 10 of the 11 licensed U.S. uranium producers. The deal required multiple approvals by the U.S., beginning with the Committee on Foreign Investments in the United States. Under federal law, the committee reviews foreign investments that raise potential national security concerns. It has nine members, including the secretaries of the treasury, state, defense, homeland security, commerce and energy; the attorney general; and representatives from two White House offices (the United States Trade Representative and the Office of Science and Technology Policy). The committee can't actually stop a sale from going through — it can only approve a sale. The president is the only one who can stop a sale, if the committee or any one member "recommends suspension or prohibition of the transaction," according to guidelines issued by the Treasury Department in December 2008 after the department adopted its final rule a month earlier.

For this and other reasons, Trump is wrong to claim that Clinton "gave away 20 percent of the uranium in the United States" to Russia. Clinton could have objected — as could the eight other voting members — but that objection alone wouldn't have stopped the sale of the stake of Uranium One to Rosatom. "Only the President has the authority to suspend or prohibit a covered transaction," the federal guidelines say.

July 28, 2017 "The previous administration enacted an open-door policy to illegal migrants from Central America. 'Welcome in. Come in, please, please.'"

The reality is Obama carried out more than 5.2 million deportations over two terms. That figure combines both "removals," which involve a formal court order, and "returns," which don't.

Obama returned more than 2 million Central Americans in his first seven years in office, according to data from the Department of Homeland Security's Office of Immigration Statistics (that does not include formal removals or 2016 data). Roughly 150,000 of those deported under Obama were returned to El Salvador, from which MS-13 hails, according to data from the Los Angeles Times. Between 2003 and 2013, one in five deportations over this time were to Central America's "Northern Triangle" countries of El Salvador, Guatemala and Honduras, some of the world's most dangerous countries, according to data analyzed by the Migration Policy Institute. Obama confronted a surge in migration from Central America, particularly from the Northern Triangle, fueled by instability, gang violence and worsening economic conditions. The Obama administration faced legal constraints -- both from a congressional statutes and court rulings -- that impeded its ability to remove an influx of illegal entrants with children, or unaccompanied minors, many of whom were fleeing Central America.

Jul 28, 2017 "We have trade deficits with almost every country because we had a lot of really bad negotiators making deals with other countries."

The United States actually has a trade surplus with more than half of the countries or governments it does business with, according to data kept by the United States International Trade Commission. These include the U. K, Brazil, Belgium, Netherlands, Singapore, Hong Kong, Saudi Arabia, Australia, Chile, Turkey, Peru, Argentina, etc.

Sept 28, 2017 "Ending the estate tax would protect millions of small businesses and the American farmer."

The Urban Institute-Brookings Institution Tax Policy Center projected that only about 80 small farms and closely held businesses would pay any estate tax in 2017. That would amount to about 1 percent of all payers of the estate tax that year. And the estate tax revenue from small businesses and farms, the center said, would amount to fifteen-hundredths of 1 percent of the total paid under the estate tax in 2017.

Oct 26, 2017 Says the GOP plan he supports is "the biggest tax cut in U.S. history."

At least six bills cut taxes by more than the current proposal. A seventh, the Revenue Act of 1978, is essentially tied with the current proposal as a percentage of GDP.

Nov 7, 2017 "Chicago is the city with the strongest gun laws in our nation."

The Law Center to Prevent Gun Violence, a pro-gun control group, gives many states higher rankings for restricting gun ownership and use. A total of seven states, including New York, Massachusetts, Connecticut, New Jersey, Maryland, California and Hawaii, have rules that go beyond what Illinois has.

Nov 30, 2017 "For years, they have not been able to get tax cuts -- many, many years, since Reagan."

That's flat wrong. Under three presidents -- Bill Clinton, George W. Bush and Barack Obama -- Congress enacted nine tax bills worth in the tens of billions of dollars in revenue reductions over four years.

The list includes the two big Bush tax cuts from 2001 and 2003, arguably the signature domestic policy achievements of his presidency. Among other things, these bills cut rates for the top bracket from 39.6 percent to 35 percent. The list also includes the extension of many of those tax cuts in advance of their scheduled expiration in 2013 under Obama -- a high-stakes legislative situation known as the "fiscal cliff."

Nov 29, 2017 "Thirteen states this year have seen unemployment drop to the lowest levels in the history of their state. And I hate to tell you, but Missouri happens to be one of them,"

The Bureau of Labor Statistics compiles the seasonally adjusted highs and lows for states, which can be found on its website. It lists 13 states that have hit historic lows this year. Not included: Missouri.

Dec 11th, 2017 "Black homeownership just hit the highest level it has ever been in the history of our country."

According to Census Bureau data, black home-ownership peaked in 2004 at 49.1 percent. It has fallen incrementally almost every year since. In fact, the rate is now about one-sixth lower than it was at its peak.

Dec 20, 2017 "They have a lottery. You pick people. Do you think the country is giving us their best people? No. What kind of a system is that? They come in by lottery. They give us their worst people, they put them in a bin, but in his hand, when he's picking them is, really, the worst of the worst. Congratulations, you're going to the United States. Okay. What a system — lottery system."

Countries don't send their people. Lottery applicants must meet minimum standards for education or work experience. The lottery is run by the United States, not foreign countries. Lottery winners are selected by a random, computerized process. Individuals must pass background vetting by the U.S. government before getting a visa. Trump's comment that the worst are coming not only ignores vetting done by the State Department, but also lottery entry requirements of at least a high school education or its equivalent, or two years of work experience within the past five years in an occupation that requires at least two years of training or experience to perform.

Dec. 27, 2017 "You know, one of the things that people don't understand — we have signed more legislation than anybody. We broke the record of Harry Truman."

In a report published on Dec. 21, 2017, govtrack.us wrote that "Trump has sunk to last place with 94 bills signed into law by his 336th day in office (today). That's eight fewer than President George W. Bush and not even half as many as presidents Bill Clinton (209) and George H.W. Bush (242)."

Jan. 18, 2018 (Twitter) "Mexico is now rated the number one most dangerous country in the world."

The only way Mexico falls first is if we only consider the International Press Institute's number of journalists who were killed in 2017. The global journalism network tallied at least 14 journalists killed in Mexico in its December 2017 report.

The main study of intentional homicides is performed by the United Nations' Office of Drug Control. The figures don't include war-related killings and deaths from internal conflicts, which are generally far higher than intentional homicides. Mexico was 10th on the list in 2015, and El Salvador was first. There were 16 intentional homicides for every 100,000 people in Mexico, whereas El Salvador had 109 per 100,000 population. (The United States, by the way, was 54th.)

This list will be updated every two weeks.

Acknowledgements: Politico Magazine, the New York Times, the Washington Post, and Politifact

Made in the USA
Coppell, TX
20 August 2020

34053080R10023